Dedicated to: All the wonderful family members who gave me the idea to make this book. Can't wait to make more magic with all y'all.Thanks, Y'all bunches!

-Josie Ann Tyler

Chapter 1

The sun just came over the mountain but I was already awake
when the sun came through my window. Well, thinking to
myself, I better get up and feed the chickens, but my mind kept
saying back to sleep, rolling over I still could not go to sleep. I
decided to get up anyway, headed to the bathroom with my
clothes in my arms. About 10 minutes later I was heading out
the sliding glass door to the back yard. Just as I got to the
chicken coop I noticed two weasels digging a hole trying as hard
as they could to get in the coop. Running back inside to grab my
slingshot, when I got back outside, I bent over to pick up a rock,
placing it in the crotch of the sling, I pulled it with all my might
hitting one of the weasels in the head. I picked it up and debated
with myself whether to make it into the stool for my mother or
not if it was even worth the hassle. I decided that it wasn't
worth it, so I just gave it to my husky to eat. I walked slowly to

the barn to pick up the bucket and grabbed the scoop filling the bucket full. I remembered I left my slingshot on the ground, leaving the bucket by the coop, making the chickens noisier because they could not get to the bucket to eat. Walking back to where I left the slingshot I bent over to grab it then ran off to where I left the bucket.

 Opening the gate slowly so no chickens could get out, I was almost done feeding the chicken when I heard a deep voice. Turning around I swear the black chicken was talking to me.

 Shaking my head and telling myself this must be a dream, no chicken can talk.

Dumping the rest of the feed on the ground, just as I was about to shut the gate once again I heard "Larry! Larry!" just as plain as day. The black chicken came closer to me and asked me to follow her.

  "Surely you can not be talking to me!" Larry said

  "Why not? Just because you never heard me before does not mean chickens can not talk. You humans just do not have the insight to listen to us animals."

  "Why talk to me now?" Larry asked.

"I have something to show you!"

In the left corner of the co-op was a pretty good size hole, I looked down and saw light coming from the hole.

 As I was staring down at the hole I kneeled to get a closer look, but when I did, something grabbed me and was pulling me through the hole I was screaming and trying to pull away, but whatever it kept pulling me more into the hole.

Finally, I landed, and to my surprise, I was in a pigpen. Coming out from the gate was a pig dressed in a suit and tie. Blinking my eyes twice I stood up.

"Where did you come from!?" Pa pig asked
Looking at the pig, I said to myself, here I go again.
Trying to speak I could not get a word out, taking a deep breath I tried again, "I came from Lebanon, Oregon."

"Where is that?"

"It's in the Northwest"
Coming up from behind me were two Piglets. They both asked at the same time,   "Who are you?"

The Papa pig said "This boy said he came from Lebanon, Oregon in the Northwest.
Papa Pig said, "Would you like some hot apple cider?"

"Wouldn't mind if I do." Said Larry.
Going into their home it was kind of cozy with a potbelly stove and wooden chairs at the table and there was a bench in the living room. There was a very small kitchen.

"Well, take a seat. Will you warm up the hot apple cider Peg? Pearl, would you bring a plate of cookies over to the table please?"Papa Pig ordered. When Papa Pig looked over at me I knew he could tell that I was very confused by all that had happened. And quite frankly I was.

"Just one minute I have something to show you. Then you will know where you are." I watched as he walked over to the bookcase and picked up a couple of books and a few pieces of paper.

As he walked back he said, "This will make it all clear to you."
Sitting the books on the table and opening a piece of paper, I
noticed it was a map.

"Have you ever read Wizard of OZ books?" Pa pig asked

"Yes." I also read Dorothy returns to OZ

"So you might remember blue is for Munchkin country
yellow is for Winkies, red is for Quadling, green is for
Emerald city and purple is for Gillikins. But other colors are not
mentioned in any of the books, but I can show you another map
that you will never see in any of the books, and I never could
understand why."

 As I was sipping the hot cider, I took too big of a gulp and
started coughing, "

"Are you okay?" Pearl asked

"Yes, I'm fine. Thank you for asking."

"Back to what I was saying. Let's take a look at the map and
you will see where you are. We are in the land of Pigment."

"Is this city all pigs?"

"Why, no. There are a lot of different things that live inland of
Pigment, but most of them are pigs."

"I thought The Wizard of Oz was just a story?"

"That's what the author wants you to believe."
We just stood looking at each other for a second, Then I asked:
"How do I get back home?"

"Well, you see you have to go to the Emerald City but, you
can not get home the same way as Dorothy. The Wizard left Tin

Man, Scarecrow, and Lion in charge of the Emerald City until the day he came back and he has not come back yet.

"So you are saying I am stuck here for the rest of my young life!"

"Don't get your tail in a straight."Papa Pig said. Then he got a look of realization "Sorry I forgot that you are a human and humans do not have tails. That is unless you are a pigman."Papa Pig said.

"A what?!?"

"I guess you've never seen a pigman before." Opening one of the books to the middle there was a picture of a pigman. The top of his body looked like a man except for the ears. They looked like a pig. The bottom part of the body looked just like a pig.
 I was surprised at what I saw, "First time for everything." I didn't realize that I had just said that until Papa Pig said

"Let's go outside and meet Mr. Fred. He's part pigman."
As I walked out the door, I could not believe my eyes. There were lots of different kinds of animals and some humans. Most of the humans were very small. Then again some of them were like giants.
Peppa Pig and I were walking away when he stopped and said: "Hi Mr. Fred how is your day going?" As he turned around he slipped on a snail and fell on top of him.
Getting back up on his hoof, the snail yelled in a loud voice "Will you watch where you put your hoof next time!" Then he crawled away. Peppa Pig didn't seem to care one bit.Mr.Fred and Papa Pig just went on with their conversation.

" Well, so far it has been a lovely day with the teal sun out. So what are you up to?"

"I would like you to meet a visitor of mine this is Larry he's from Lebanon, Oregon." The snail, hearing that I came from a far off place, turned around.

"You say what! I've never heard of this place before." Mr.Fred exclaimed.

"Let's have a seat and I will explain." After Papa pig got done telling him about me, Mr.Fred just laughed. And I learned the name of the snail, just in case you were wondering. His name is Sammy. Let's get back to my story.
Sammy asked, "Are you related to Dorothy of Kansas?"

"No. I thought Dorothy was just made up for the story."

"You humans are so funny," Sammy replied
I looked about and was shocked at what I saw. There were just not pigs in this town. There were half pig, half-humans.
Coming down the street was the tallest man I'd ever seen. He had long black curly hair and a star tattoo on his forehead.
I asked Fred who this man was.

"He's one of the misfits of the town. The school teacher found him on the school steps so she took him in as her son." Replied Pa pig

"I thought this town was only pigs or pigment? Why is Sammy here?"

"He ran away from his family because they wanted him to marry the ugliest snail in the town of Snailville.

"Where do I go from here so I can get back home?"I asked

"See that yellow brick road? You have to follow it. There are lots of yellow brick roads that go to different parts of Oz. You need to keep going till you get to Emerald City." Replied Papa Pig.

 Waving goodbye, I was on my own and hoping I would get there safe.

After a while I had been walking for so long it seemed like I was going nowhere. All I was seeing was field after field of different colored sunflowers.

 Just when I thought I was going nowhere, there in front of me was a sign that said, 'Sunflower Villa' with an arrow pointing to the right. But to the left, there was no arrow. Looking both ways, I could not decide which road to take. It was getting late so I decided to spend the night. I sat down on a stump. Boy, it gets cold out here at night and before I knew it, I saw a sleeping bag and pillow by my feet. Blinking my eyes to see if I was just dreaming I found out that they were real. So I grabbed the sleeping bag and pillow and found a patch of grass to sleep on.

Chapter 2

When I woke up I could smell bacon and eggs cooking. I looked around me, but I could not see where the smell was coming from.

I looked down and the sleeping bag and pillow were nowhere to be found. I thought that was odd. I remembered the road that I was trying to decide on whether I should take the left or the right road.

I decided to take the road to the right, so off I went on my merry way. Just about then I came upon a cottage that looked strange. The siding of the house was made up of sunflower seeds. I saw a little boy and I waved. He waved back and said "Good day to you, sir. The little boy was wearing bib overalls that had a sunflower in the middle of the pocket on the bib.

"Good day to you also," I said

"Never saw you around here before." replied the small boy

"No, I'm from Lebanon, Oregon."

"Never heard of that city before." replied the small boy

Just then a lady came to the door yelling for someone named Sunny, "I gotta go my mom is calling me." The boy named Sunny said

"Bye," I replied.

Walking away I heard someone call "Would you like to have breakfast with us?" I looked around to see who was talking to me. I realized that it was Sunny's mom. I looked around once more just to make sure that she was talking to me."Sure."I said replying to the lady of the house.

Coming into the house I notice a Siamese cat was lying on the rug by the fireplace.

Sitting at the head of the table was a grey-haired man with long sideburns, he had the same bib overalls as the little boy did. In a deep sounding voice, I heard.

"Take a load off your feet"

Pulling out the chair I took a seat and folded my hands in my lap because I was nervous.

"What's your name, young man?" Asked the man at the table.

I was so nervous I stuttered as I said my name 'La-Larry'.

"Very nice to meet you." The man put his hand out so that I could shake it. And I did."We do not get many strangers in this land."The man said.

As we carried on our conversation, the lady of the house put down a big plate of eggs and bacon along with toast. After she sat down the head of the house said the morning prayer.

"Guest First." the lady of the house said.

After I got my food, I said to the man, "I never got your name."

"No you did not this is my wife Flower and you met my son, Sunny. I'm Johnny. Well, tell me a little bit about yourself." so I began to tell him my story. Partway through the story, I picked up my fork and took a big bite of the eggs, "These chicken eggs taste different than the eggs back home."

"They're, not chicken eggs, they're chiduck," replied Flower

"Does that mean they are duck and chicken?"

"Yep."

"Let's finish the story," Johnny said

"So that is how I got to where I am now," I said after I finished my story. After they all finished Breakfast and we men decided to sit on the porch for a while before I had to be on my way once again.

After some time talking I finally said my goodbyes and started on my journey once again.

Chapter 3

Thinking about my journey I had so far, this is a strange place. I was wondering if Mom and Dad were looking for me or if my brother and sisters are happy I'm gone. They most likely were quite pleased that I was not around to annoy them.

Still, the only thing that I've seen so far is more and more sunflowers and small cottages.
Just as I thought the sunflowers would never end, I came across orchards of trees that had pies hanging where you would think peaches or other fruit would be hanging on the branches of the trees.

I was so hungry that I reached up and grabbed one of the pies and sat under the tree. I took a small bite because I did not know if It would Taste like pie.

I could not believe how good it was. It tasted like lemon and lime with a hint of cinnamon. The crazy thing was that you could even eat the pie plate.

I jumped to my feet and pulled another pie off the tree. This time the pie was different. It was orange cream. My favorite.

By the time I got done with the sixth pie I was so full, I could hardly move.

I fell asleep under the tree and did not wake until the next morning. That's when I heard a car coming down the yellow brick road. I turned my head to get a better look. It was the strangest thing. It was a part motorcycle and part Ford. The front was the front of a motorcycle in the back was the back of the Ford truck. I thought he was going to go right past me when he pulled to the side of the road.

He noticed me right after he got off the motorcycle. I was still looking when he came around and started to walk up the incline. As soon as he got right in front of me I looked him in the eye. I was a little bit scared right then and wished I was back home again.

"What are you doing in my orchard? Don't just stand there like a lump of clay! Answer my question!" said the man. His name, by the way, was Ruben.

"I came about your orchard when I was walking and noticed the pie tree, I didn't think I was that hungry until I saw them, I did not notice that they belong to anybody."

"Well, you should have!"

I was tumbling with fear, didn't know what this man would do to me. "I'm very sorry sir."

   "I'll let it slide this time but don't let it happen again!"

   "Yes, sir. It won't."

So I took off in a flash and didn't stop until I came to a creek. Boy was I thirsty. I just need a little drink, but how do I know this creek does not belong to someone else.

Just then I heard a voice

Saying hi then I notice a little red-haired girl in pigtails. She reminded me of Tom Sawyer with that red hair and straw hat on.

   "I never saw you around here before, you must be new."

   "How do you know I'm new here?"

   "Because everyone in Red River has red hair."

   "I got lost in my backyard through a hole in the ground and ended up here."

   "Do you mean you came up from the ground, here in Red River?"

   "No, no, I fell into this hole on my parent's farm when I was talking to a chicken and before you knew it, I was in Pigment Land."

   " We study about Pigment land in school. Where are you heading to now?" Boy does she talk fast.

   "One of the pigs that I met in Pigment Land, Papa pig, told me to take the yellow brick road to the Emerald City to see if I can get help finding my way back home."

   "You sure are being a smart mouth kid. Are you sure you're on the right path of the yellow brick road?"

"You know I'm not quite sure myself. I've been walking and walking and I just don't know anymore," I said.

She just stared at me with these bright blue eyes and had an odd look on her face. All I cared about was getting there safe. After taking my last sip of water and washing my face, I told her I must be on my way so I can make it. "It was very nice to meet you."

"Likewise."

Boy, this place is a lot different than where I come from, there are so many strange things going on here.

I came to another turning point in the road, it had three signs on the post, to your left the sign said, Butterfly Lane. the one pointing straight ahead said Frogvillie the one to the right said Anchor, boy this would be fun to ride in a boat and see all different size boats.

So I made my decision to go to Anchor but I did not see what I thought I would see.

When I got to the town there was no boat insight I keep looking but all I saw were people with box cameras and many other types of cameras and notepads.

I came across this old man with a grey cane, sir, where are all the different boats to ride.

He coughed twice and in a high voice replied: "you mixed this town up with Anchorville."

I looked at him with a puzzled look I did not understand what he meant.

  And he could tell I was confused, "Well, laddie let me explain there are two towns there's one that has boats and its called Anchorville, the other town is Anchor and that where Anchormen and Anchor Women and news reporters live this is the head of the news world here for all parts of Oz and surrounding areas.

Chapter 4

I thanked the old man and went on my way checking out this town. On one of the street corners, I saw a young boy holding up a newspaper yelling."Get your top news from the Corner Circle!"Also, I saw lots of places to buy coffee on the streets or in coffee houses.

This must be what it looks like on Wall Street, So much traffic also, the buildings were so tall here I felt like I was in my dream city I always want to go to New York.

From the time I was little, I knew I wanted to be a writer and work for a top newspaper. People always laugh at me because I was only 10 and they would tell me you will change your mind a dozen times in your life before you are 19 years old as what type of job you want.

Looking across the street I saw a park with a playground and other kids playing decide to go over and play, when I got there I noticed the way they were dressed, it looked like they came from the 1800's It did not bother me the way they were dressed.

"Hi, what you are doing," a little girl came over and asked me," I just came over to play a little bit before I go on my journey again."

"Where you going," She sure asked lots of questions, I explain to her what I was doing here she looked at me and turned around and waved to the other children to come and hear my story.

When they all arrived she said he's a good storyteller please tell them the story you told me.

"It's not a story it did happen this way!"So once again I told them my story as the children sat on the ground and listen with joy.

One little boy was waving his arm in the air, I asked him if he needed to use the restroom and all the kids just broke out laughing.

"What's so funny?"

"You," they all said.

"When is the storybook coming out?"

They still did not get this wasn't a story!!!!!

I felt a tap on my shoulder turning around a middle-aged woman said: "This is a story it's like a story of part of your life, people can make anything into a story, and it sounds mighty good you should consider writing a book when you get back home about it."

"I never thought about it."

When I turned back around all the kids had left me and were once again playing on the playground.

I walked over and climbed up the ladder and went down the longest slide I have ever been on before.

It was getting much later than I thought I need to get going or I will never make it on my journey.

I saw lots of things I never have seen before like a camel walking on the shoulder of the street with two people riding it like you would a horse.

Also coming down the road was a motorcycle that looked like a hog. To my surprise it was pearl one of the papa pig daughter's I waved and she saw me and did a U-turn right in front of the horse-drawn buggy scared the living daylights out of both horses they started, running so fast the old man couldn't keep hold of the reins.

If it wasn't for me running at top speed and grabbing the reins and pulling for the horses to stop the buggy would have run right into the candy store.

Turning around I ask the old man if he was okay.

"Yep thanks for saving my life, Let me buy you some 2 cents candy."

I never heard of this kind of candy before, well I followed right behind him, the bell went off that was above the door.

To my surprise, there were shelves after shelves and bins full of candy,

"Hi, Mr. Brown how can I help you today?"

"I would like 2 cents of gumdrops for my new friend."

"Do you want your regular?"

"Yes please!"

I watched Mr. Brown take out his coin purse and gave the clerk
two shining 2 cent coins.
   "I ask the clerk what is a 2 cent coin look like?"
    "You never saw one before." replied the clerk.
   "No sir I have not," Larry replied
    "Give me your hand." the clerk replied.
He placed the coin in my hand I took my other hand and picked
the coin up and checked it out, to my surprise it looked almost
like a penny, "   "Here you go Mr."
   "And here you go young fellow. Replied the clerk
I could not believe my eyes when he handed it to me the brown
paper was in the shape of a cone and the gumdrops where place
inside like you would have in an ice cream cone.
   "Thanks." Sir
Mr. Brown had a big smile on his face when he looked at me he
was enjoying watching me have so much fun, He handed a sack
to Mr. Brown and you could see red, black and blue licorice
from the top of his sack.
   "Boy, you sure get a lot of candy for 2 cents."
    "The clerk asks where are you from?"
taking a deep breath I told him.
    "So you are going all the way to Emerald City to see the
Wizard, I'm sorry to tell you but he left in a hot air balloon
meaning years ago.
  But maybe the Lion, Scarecrow, and Tinman can help you get
back home the Wizard put them in charge when he left till the
day he comes back."

"I sure hope so I gotta get back home mom and dad are probably wondering what happens to me."

"Why not take a look around my store and you can pick out another kind of candy to take on your journey."
Across the way was a mirror with a counter and stools like you would see in the old Western movies in the Saloon.
But children and adults were drinking soda pop and rootbeer floats.
I saw a box of soap on a lower shelf and wondering to myself why would a box of soap be in the candy store.
Someone came up behind me to stack more soapboxes on the shelf.

"May I ask you something?" Sir

"Go ahead." Stock boy side

"Why would a candy store carry a box of soap?"

"He could not help but laugh at me, "What's so funny!"

"If you would have read the whole box you would have seen what it said Soap Flake Candy, I can give you a sample to try."
I was kind of afraid to try it but I took my chance, the stock boy put a little dab on my hand and said now you lick it off after I did this I was surprised to see how much I like the taste of soap candy. I started to walk away but I keep thinking of the soap candy should I pick this candy or just keep looking I decide to keep looking to see if there was something better, but what could be better than soap flakes.
I saw gummy dogs as big as me, should I pick them but I walked by, the clerk was watching me enjoying myself after seeing all I

saw I went back to pick up the soap candy walking up to the clerk I showed him what I picked.

"Well, you have a safe trip, and would you like to take one more soap candy box home with you so you can show your family this type of candy."

"Sure!" Thanks
I ran back to get the soap candy I picked up the last soap candy box and went back to pick up the other.

"Let me put them in a sack for you."
The sack was not paper it was cloth and big enough to put more things in it.

"I told the clerk and Mr, Brown thanks and off I went hoping I would get there soon."
I keep walking not slowing down tell I saw the edge of town with a sign saying leaving Anchor to come again.

Chapter 5

Waiting for me at the edge of the town was pearl the pig.

"I thought you would never get out of this town." Pearl the pig said.

"Why not?" Larry Asked

"Because it took you so long." Pearl the pig replied.

"Well, What are you doing from Pigment?" asked Larry.

"I'm going to pick up my Papa yearly supply of medication for his leg cramps. I gotta drive thru the dessert before I can get to Pharmacia, would you like me to give you a ride, it's a lot faster than walking and much cooler.

Pearl grabbed hold of my hand to help me get on the motorcycle and we went down the yellow brick road.

On each side of the road were sand and cacti that all you could see for miles and miles

"Good thing you came along or I would be walking in all this heat," Larry said.

As we were both talking along came a snake slithering in the middle of the road, Pearl honks the horn but the snake would not move, just as the motorcycle came upon the snake the front wheel of the motorcycle hit the middle of the snake sending it in the air to the other side of the road with a thump it landed in a pile of sand.

The motorcycle came to a complete stop and we both could not help but laugh.

"Well, Larry what do you think sofar of Oz?"
"It sure not like anyplace I ever saw in my life, each area is so different."
"Well that the fun part of living in Oz, and getting to know the people and see new people come here."
"Where is Dorothy?" asked Larry
"I'm not sure, she could be anywhere she travels a lot and visits friends and family."
Starting up the motorcycle we were on our way once again with the wind blowing in my face, I was wondering to myself how come we do not see anybody else driving by, but before I knew it, a Jackrabbit came by on a bike, Pearl waved and we left the Jack Rabbit in the dust. I was so thirsty my tongue was dry as sand, I Just wish I had a cool limeade to drink that mom made.
"Hay do you see what I see, there a gas station, restaurant, and a hotel and two small dome size homes, they were never here before." Pearl, the pig said loudly.
"Are you sure Pearl?"
"Course I'm sure! I have been riding this road seen I was 14 years old." Replied Pearl
"I thought teenagers had to be 16 years old to drive."
"Remember you are in Oz and we have different laws then were you come from all teenagers here must be 14 years of age and have never been in trouble with the law and are in 8th grade

if you decide to drop out of school you will not be able to drive tell you to turn 21."

 "I wish we had a law like this back home," said Larry.
Pearl slowly turned the motorcycle into the gas station driving up to the pump, out came a beetle in bib overalls, that was a sight to see for both uses.
In a southern drawl "How may I be of service?"
I need $4.00 worth of gas please." replied Pearl

   "I never saw a gas station, restaurant, or anything before in the desert." Pearl Said.

   "No you have not the black beetles just got tired of living with all the different other types of beetles and we wanted to start our city."

   "Where are all the other beetles?" Asked Larry

   "They are over on the other side of the road-building their dome home and the town, we are thinking of having a bridge built from one side to the other side of the road."

   "What is the name of this town?" Asked Larry

 "We have two names picked out Bettleland or Bettlevilla we are going to have a town meeting tonight to see what name we should use than we have to send 6 of the top leaders to Emerald City to fill out paperwork and have the wizard of Oz sign the paperwork but because he not here we have to get the Tinman or lion to sign the paperwork saying the names okay and why should there be another city in Oz."

 "How come you want to start your own city? Asked Larry

"Well being a black beetle we get the short end of the stick with less pay and not the best of the job either and some places we are not allowed to go because of the color of our shell.

"That awful." replied both Larry and Pearl.

"We want to build a statue of the first Battle for the center of the town with a plaque telling the history of the town and when it became a town.

"Sounds like a wonderful Idea and we both wish you the best of luck," replied Pearl

"Pearl reached into her wallet and pulled out a $4.00 coin and handed it to the beetle.

"Do you have a drinking fountain?" Asked Larry

"Right around the corner of the building." replied the beetle Larry jump of the motorcycle as fast as he could and dashed the fountain.

Coming behind him was pearl waiting for her drink as well, "Okay Larry save some water for me she laughed."

So off they went with a wave goodbye, "How long till we get out of the desert." Asked Larry

"a full day and full night if I keep driving all night, I think I will drive for two more hours, then we can stop and sleep."

"But where?"

"In the tent, I have in the box on the back of the motorcycle."

"Oh!"

"Let's put the radio on for the news." Turning the dial to find the news Pearl was having trouble finding a station because being out in the desert there was no good reception.

Pearl stopped the motorcycle and pulled over as we listened to the news and getting the tent set up for the night.

"This is James the Emerald City news report we are coming live from the apple orchard that threw the apple at Dorothy when she first came to Oz, well bets all things they are doing it again but not at Dorothy this time it looks to be like the great Oz came back, let's see if we can have a word with him, "can I interview you for are radio news broadcast," James asked

"Why would you want to interview me?" The man asked

"You are the Great Oz that has made his way back to the people," James said.

"With a chucker, he just looked at me for a second, and finally spoke I'm not the great Oz you must be referring to my great great grandfather."

"You look so much like him." Said, James

"You may interview me, " The man said

"How did you get here?" Asked James

"I was at the carnival and decide to have some fun with a friend of mine so we went into the House of Mirrors where you have to find your way out, halfway through the House of Mirrors saw a bright light and thought it was the exit. Instead, the bright light came closer and closer tell it covered my whole body, and before you knew it, here I am." Replied the man.

"So where is your great great great grandfather?" Asked James

"He's back in Kansas working for the carnival I always thought this place he talked about was a story he made up." Replied the man

"So are you going to take over the Emerald City and be another great Oz?" Asked James

"Well, I never gave it much of a thought when I always thought it was a story he just made up." Replied the man.

"I forgot to ask what your name is," James asked

"Peter"

"You heard it from James the Emerald City radio news reporter well keep you updated on this news story."

Chapter 6

Peter said goodbye and started on his way.

"Peter!" Wait just one minute, How would you like to ride back in my Helicopter."
Turning slowly around Peter eyed me with his big green eyes and a smile that could light up an entire room.

"I always wanted to ride in a Helicopter!" Peter replied.

Both walked towards, the Helicopter, when out of nowhere a rabbit jumped out of a hole it startled both of us.
Pushing the starter button the engine choked with a cloud of black smoke coming from the engine, we both looked at each other wondering what was going wrong.
Jumping out of the Helicopter I opened the hood and to my surprise, the bunnies were eating the cord that goes to the battery, I picked them both up and threw them to the ground.
Going back inside the Helicopter I started looking for duck tape hoping this would hold the cord tell I got back to Emerald City.
Pushing the starter button it choked again, but Eventually, it started lifting us off the ground.

When we got to the attitude we needed I looked out the window, all I saw was sand and hills of sand, "I asked the reporter does anybody live here in the desert?"

"Why yes, we have the Sand king, and there a village of homes made out of the sand.

With a puzzled look on my face, I thought he was joking with me.

"I see by the exception on your face you do not believe me." Said, James.

"Well, it's kind of hard to believe," Peter said.

"Why?" James asked

"Because sand gets muddy when it gets wet." Replied Peter.

"Here in Oz we have a different kind of rain over the desert, and it never does muddy the sand. It might look like the regular rain but the dessert is the only place that gets this type of rain." James replied.

"That is so cool!" Peter said

"We will be coming up on SandyLand in a couple of minutes, it right over the sand dunes," James said

As we got closer to SandyLand we both could see the bright lights coming from the town.

Just as we were over the town the Helicopter started choking again, James was thinking to myself we are going to crash into the water tower.

The helicopter did a nose dive and the nose of the helicopter hit the sand about a foot away from the water tower sending sand up into the air and landing on the water tower, Just as we both looked up you could see cops coming at us with sticks.

"Come on out of there!!" Yelling all twelve cops.

We got out very slowly not knowing what they might do to us,
We both had a strange look on our face.
The chief came closer asking us who we were and what are you
doing here.
  With a soft voice, I answered him "I'm a James reporter from
the Emerald City and this is Peter he's new here.
  "Well look what you did to are water tower!" The Chief said.
  "I'm so sorry didn't mean for it to happen." Said, James
  "Well you did now we got to take you to see the Sand King."
Peter looked over at the reporter and he gave me a sorry look,
but I was too scared to even talk.
  "Move the chief," he said in a loud voice.
 as the other cops behind us keep poking us with their sticks, we
were both looking around us as the sand people were starting to
come out of their sandstone homes, Peter thought this reminded
me of the sand you put in bottles at the fairgrounds.
We started going over one dune and below it was the tallest
cactus I ever saw they were as big as the evergreens back home.
  "Whispered to James where are they taking us?" Peter asked
  "They talked about a sand king," James replied
  "Quiet no talking!" The Chief said.
I did not see the yellow brick road that my grandfather always
talked about that Dorothy took. I knew I was lost for sure, with a
tear rolling down my cheek, I was wishing with all my might
that I was back at the carnival with my grandfather.
  "Don't cry Peter everything will be alright you will see,"
James said

"Know it won't I come to a strange land that I always thought was just a make-believe place in grandfather stories now look where I am," said Peter
Scratching my chest I forgot that I still had my tape recorder going, as I did I moved my patch crocked.
We made it to the castle, one of the cops pulled out a set of keys from his pocket and placed it in the lock, a couple of seconds later the drawbridge open up and we were walking into the castle.

Chapter 7

I was still awake and could not fall asleep because Pearl was snoring so loudly. But at least I had the radio to listen to. I was still listening to the news, it was more like a story about these people's adventure.

The castle was much colder than outside, down the hall, you could see the king's throne, but no king was sitting upon it.

All at once, you could hear thunder and drums, and then from the side door outwalked the king, with his tan cape and cactus crown, walking over to the throne he place himself upon it.

"What do we have here?"Asked the king.

The chief walked up to the throne, and told him exactly what had happened, the king ponders over this for a little while."

"What do you both have to say for yourself?"

"Well you see I'm James one of the reporters from Emerald City and we had a news story on the apple tree they were throwing apples at someone, I knew it could not be Dorothy because she has been living here for some time and I've not heard them doing this to her again. From A distance I thought I saw the Great Oz walking down the yellow brick road but when I got closer I still thought it was him until I ask the young man about this and he told me he was the great-great-grandson of the great Oz."

The king looked over at Peter and asked him if this was true. replying in a soft voice Peter said "Yes."

"Let me sleep on this and I will give you my decision after breakfast, take them and lock them up in the tower for the night and give them a glass of milk and grapes for dinner."

"We both followed the cops out of the throne room turn towards the steps up to the towers, Peter and James could not believe how many steps they had to climb to get to the towers. The Chief pulled the key from his pocket to unlock the door but had the wrong one, so he tried another key, and this time it worked.
We both were afraid to walk into the room, it was so dark the only light in the room was coming in from a tiny window.
 The night seemed to go on forever, as we both were sitting in the corner of the room.
Pearl woke up to the radio, "Are you still listening to the news?"
 "Sure am! You should have been listening." Larry replied
 "Why?" Pearl Asked
Because you miss out on lots of great adventures the two people were having." Larry said.
 "How can news be so exciting?"   Pearl the pig asked.
"Well it just is, you will have to listen to it when they play it again," Larry replied
 The sun was slowly coming up, "We should be on our way or I will never get Papa's pills, and you need to get to Emerald City.
On our ride to where Pearl was driving, we were listening to the news story when out of the blue we could hear footsteps coming

closer and closer. We both did not know who it was or what would happen next. We could hear the key turning in the lock and slowly the door opened up with a creaking sound that made Peter jump up.

 We both got on our feet in a flash we moved up by the window so we could get a better look because the sun rays were to shine through the tiny window.

 One of the cops said," The chief is talking to the king about what to do with you two. Come on, Let's not dawdle."
Taking two steps at a time we made it down faster than when we were going up to the tower.

  "It's about time you got here!!" with an angry face the king said

  "I decided to have you sweep all the sand and wash down the water tower before I even think about letting you go."

  "But I need to get back to Emerald City Radio I'm the news report."

 "I do not care what you are, you dirted up the water tower you have to clean it, then I will have someone look at your Helicopter and help you fix it."
So before we knew it we were cleaning the water tower finally got done with all the sweeping, but they would not let us go wait till tomorrow. So again we were going back to the castle tower to sleep.

Chapter 8

Pearl pulled up to the pharmacy, "I thanked her for the ride."
"You just keep going straight down the yellow brick road and you will get there soon," Pearl said.
I waved goodbye as I was walking, I keep thinking about Peter and James, wanted to know what happened, it made me want to get to Emerald City faster so I could find out.
 As I was walking it seems like I was going nowhere at all, I'll have seen was wheat field after wheat field, Boring.
Turning the corner I saw lots of people reading books and doing word search puzzles.
My sisters at home would love this town, they are always reading something and doing word search puzzles, But the strangest thing was that I never saw the name of the town. As I was walking I stopped in front of a big window in the middle of the window was a hardback book called The Life and time of Dorothy Standing next to me was a little girl must have been around 8 years old.
 I turned to ask her, "Is this the true story of Dorothy that came from Kansas."
  "Are you talking to me?" The girl replied.
   "Yes, do you see anybody else around here?" Larry said
   "Why yes, this book is about Dorothy Gail that came from Kansas." the girl said

I have been trying to save up money so I can buy this book."
 "Why not just get the book from your local library?"
She just looked at me for a second and then spoke to me.
"You can not get a new book from Library tell the Library queen
says it can be in the library, and most of the time it can be 2 to 5
years before she will say yes." The girl replied
    "Why do you need to have a queen over all the libraries,
    "You must never have heard of Library land or you would not
have asked."
    "I thought everyone in Oz new about this town, where have
you been all your life?"
    "I'm not from around here I'm from the city of Lebanon,"
replied Larry
    "Well, I never heard of this place in Oz." The girl said.
    "It's not in Oz it in the city of Lebanon," Larry replied
    "Do they have Libraries where you come from?" The girl
asked.
    "They do, but not as many as you have in one town," Larry
said.
On the other side of me was a teenage boy, he heard our
conversation and started talking to me.
    "We have different types of libraries like the one behind you
is Art library down on 2nd street is the kids' library Also on 23rd
is the adult library, The History library is just around the corner
to my right. Also, we have a cartoon library, Magazine library,
and a private library that has a tea room and coffee room this

library you have pay yearly to use, also we have about ten different book stores in town."

"Boy the people living in this town must read a lot, How come you do not have a sign saying the name of your town?" Aske Larry

"They are fixing the sign it was blowing over in a bad wind storm about two weeks ago and speaking of the sign here it comes the Army is carrying the sign. "Replied the teenage boy I finally got to learn the name of this Town Library land, I should have Guessed what the town would be called.

"May I ask why do you need a private library?" Asked Larry

"Because the rich people do not like to go to the same library the average person goes to." replied the girl I thought to myself that I should stay in this town and look at all the different libraries before heading to Emerald City, but if I do then my mother and father would think I'm lost and never coming home.

Leaving the outside of the book store I started walking down the sidewalk, a couple of blocks later I saw a sign saying coming soon Cookbook library boy if we had a library like this one back home my mother would be down there all the time, just thinking of the cookbooks I did not know how much I miss my mother cooking tell just now, as a tear come down my cheeks.

Out of the corner of my eye, I saw a kid playing with matches lighting them and just throwing them on the grounded I looked around to see if I could spot a cop, but none in sight, before I knew it I saw sparks flying than other people started yelling.

"Fire! Fire! At the Cartoon library!"
The yelling was like a tidal wave explosion happening, then out of nowhere came a siren with two black horses pulling a wagon more than one wagon coming down the street, but each wagon had two black horses, one of the wagons had a white dog with pink spots all over it, this reminds me of the dalmations we have back home at the fire stations but ours had black spots.
There was a crowd of people standing around watching the firemen trying to put the fire out but was not having any luck at that point. It grew bigger and bigger till it hit the next block and was inflaming the Apartment building, it took most of the day for the firemen to put the fire out. I was so busy watching that I did not hear the person behind me, asking me to move over, I got a tap on my shoulder asking me to move over so the news reporter could get a picture of the apartment under fire.
After about 10 minutes they had the fire completely out.
 I turned around and walked away but I still decided, I must be on my way, but every time I did something came up and I wanted to see what was going on in this town.
 I was starting to get thirsty but had no money to buy anything, came upon a drinking fountain but the strangest thing was that you had to pay for drinking 2 cents for a couple of gulps then under that was for a minute drink it cost you 3 cents, I was looking around to see if anybody had dropped any money but not my luck. Just as I was leaving a little person came up to me, "You look like you are thirsty I have 2centst you can have she dropped the money in the side of the fountain and I took my two

gulps of water it felt so good going down my throat, I looked her in the eyes and "thank her."

"My Plager."

I was almost out of this town and being just a kid, I leaped to see if I could jump past the sign that said thanks for visiting the town I almost made it but fell on my butt stood u,p and brushed the dirt off my pants off on another part of my adventure.

Thinking back on my adventures, one thing I wish I could do is finishing listening to the news about the Emerald City news reporter and Peter the great-great-great-grandson and their adventures.

Soon it will be getting dark, I need to find a place to sleep I guess before I sleep I will find a blanket or sleeping bag, but this time it was not my luck.

I came upon a log and decided to use the log as my pillow so I leaned up against it and scooted down tell my head was leaning against the log.

Chapter 9

When I awoke the next morning, to my surprise again I found a blanket covering me.

Now I would just like to know how I keep getting covered with a blanket or sleeping bag when there is nobody around me.

I had no clue what I was going to eat for breakfast, once I stood up I noticed the blanket was gone. Bushing myself off and taking the comb from my back pocket, and combing my hair hoping it was in place.

I notice across the road was a bush and it looked like it had toast on the bush, blinking and shaking my head I started towards the bush.

When I got there a part of the bush had toast with butter on it the other part has some kind of jam on the toast.

I did not know which one to try first so I close my eyes and spin around once and put my hand out and picked a piece of toast from the bush it was one with jam on it, I wonder what it tastes like.

" Why not give it a try." said a small voice

 I looked around but did not see anybody tell something pulled on my pant leg.

I looked behind me and to my amazement, I notice a very very little person she was the size of a pea I bent down and scooped her up into my hand.

"Well you please be so kind as to put me down on the leaf of the bush." replied the pea-size lady.
I did as she asked me to do, I just could not believe a person could be so small and still be alive.
"May I ask who you are and why you did not ask me before you took the toast of the bush?" Replied the pea-size lady
"I just thought I would have one piece of toast and whoever owned it would not miss it," Larry said in a low voice
"Well I do!" said the pea-size lady
 "Would you like it back?" Replied Larry
"I shall say not, you already touched it!" replied the pea size lady
I just remembered about the pie tree that happened last time I took something that was not mine in Oz.
 "I should not have touched," said Larry
 "I never saw you in this part," replied the pea size lady
 "I'm not from around here I come from Upper Berlin DR." Replied Larry
I finally took a bite of the small toast the jam tasted like blackberry Also the toast was the size of the kid's cereal and the brushes were the sizes of dwarf trees.
 After swallowing the toast, I looked around but didn't see any homes, or town
"Where your town?" asked Larry
 "Do you see the yellow flowers over there?" ask the pea size lady.
"Yes!" replied Larry

"We live under these flowers under all this sandy." replied the pea size lady.

"So what do you do with all the toast on the bushes?" asked Larry.

"We harvest them for all the people that live in Oz and the surrounding area, we keep some for us." replied the pea size lady.

"I sure wish I could see your city but I'm too big to go down under all the sandy." I was sounding so pitifully it wasn't funny at all.

"Just you wait a minute let me see if the mayor will let you come to our city. Replied the pea-size lady.

Before I could get the words out she was off in a flash, know where to be found as far as my eyes took me all I could see was sand and toast bushes.

I took one last look back before I open the door to the main flower that would take me to the mayor's home, today people new not to bug the mayor it was his fishing day he was getting ready to go, but what choice did I have if I wanted him to see my city, sitting down I push myself inside one of the roots and was off before you knew it, I was standing at the mayor's door. I knocked twice the door open slowly standing in front of me was the butler.

"May I help you." The butler asked

"I need to see the mayor please." Asked the pea-size lady

"Sorry he not seeing anybody today, I thought everyone knew today was the mayor fishing day and he was not to be bugged." Replied the butler.

"Coming down the last step who was that at the door?" The Mayor asked.

Some child that wanted to see you but I remind her that today was your fishing day." Sir

Going quickly to the door but when I reach out for the doorknob the butler put his hand on my shoulder.

"Kindly please remove your hand."

"But Sir, before I could finish the mayor, was talking."

"I know you were just doing your job but the people of this town are my responsibility even if it's a child that wants to see me.

I was walking down the cobblestone when the mayor came upon me.

"Dear child, may I help you?" Asked the mayor

I turned around with a sad look on my face, "Why look so sad my child."

"I was going to ask if I could bring someone down here to see the town, he was new to the area." said the pea-size lady.

"Come take a seat on my step." replied the mayor

We both sat down with a smile on his face, "now would explain to me about the new person. Said the mayor

I told him exactly what happened and he ponders over what I was telling him.

"Now I see I'm not sure it would be safe to let a stranger into our lovely town we do not know much about him do we."

"No! Sir

"So please go back up and let the person know he can not come into our city unless he gets a letter from the Emerald City passport office letting him into our city, off you go now," said the mayor.

So once again I was going up the roots and next thing you know I was back in front of the boy.

"Well what did the Mayor say!" replied the Larry

"He told me to let you know that you have to go to the Emerald City to passport office you need a letter saying it's okay for you to come to our town. And when you do get the letter to bring it over to the boulder by the yellow flower and then they will let you in, let them know you want to see Flower."

"But I can see the flowers from on top of the hill," I replied I could not understand why she was laughing at what I just said. "What so funny!!" Larry said.

"I'm sorry for laughing at you but Flower is my name."
"I'll see you around.", and with that, I walked away and down the yellow brick road once again.

Chapter 10

Back home my sisters and brother were just getting ready to start morning chores, They didn't even know I was missing yet.

Mom was still in her room doing what she does every morning doing the paperwork for her small shop and she always read her Bible first thing in the morning before starting her day and then she would read her romance novel she always reads a chapter a day.

My younger brother Frederick was just getting ready to take a shower because some mornings he wets his bed still.

Darla my youngest sister that wakes up early was doing the thing she does best every morning by yelling as she playing.

My second to the oldest sister was doing what she does almost every morning she was the last one out of bed because she would not wake up or she would be reading, and mom would always have to tell Josie to get up.

My other sister Blair was always reading every morning before taking a shower.

Last but not least there my sister Abigaile most of the time she would be reading or doing a word search puzzle before slithering out of bed.

Then there's the head of the family My dad, Jake, he was up before anybody, getting ready to go to work, he worked at the college.

It made me so sad to think how much I miss my family, tears were willing up in both eyes.

 I almost forgot about my cousin Tammy that living with us she was almost up every day before us, she volunteered at mom's shop, and at the church food bank. She is living with us because she has epilepsy and does not drive plus she a widow, most of the time I like having her around, she has a deer head Chihuahua that's a service dog.

 A couple of months ago we had Albert come and stay with us he's 20 his parents are missionaries to the Philippines, he is learning how to become an adult mom says he got a job in a factory boxing food up, but one thing I like about him the most is that he likes to play basketball with me.

 I was crying so hard now that I could not see in front of me so I took a load off by sitting on the big rock.

One thing I was glad of that my sisters, brother, and Albert could not see me crying this much they would be calling me a baby.

"I need to get home!!!!"Yelling at the top of my lungs. They all came inside after hours of doing chores, mom was making her famous blueberry flapjacks for breakfast.

As she turned around she asks if we all got chores done and she kept looking but could not find Larry.

 "Has anybody seen Larry this morning?" Mom asked
We all said, "No!"
"I wonder where he is? You all go outside and look for him and look down at the creek." Mom said

"Oh, mom!" Josie said with a grumpy look.

"Can't we look for him after we eat breakfast?" Blair replied

"No one is getting breakfast till you find him Move," mom Yelled.

The last one out was Abigail she slammed the door so hard all the hinges came off and the door fell back and hit the piano.

Reba came running out to see if Tammy had a seizure.

"Reba go back and get on your pillow," replied Tammy

Connie came running from the kitchen forgetting to turn the stove off. "Abigaile you come right back here you hear me!"

Abigaile was stomping her feet as she came upon the porch and into the house.

"Look what you have done I never want to see you do this again do you hear me!"

Abigaile was staring at the floor and wiggling about, not even looking up.

"Look at me, not the floor! You are grounded from going to the pool party and sleepover you will do all your brother and sister chores for a month plus sweep the front and back porch off today every day you will be up at 5:00 am starting chores, also you will be pulling all the weeds from the garden for a month tomorrow you will clean the van out.

I want you to also clean the bathroom up this afternoon, and no movies for a month and early to bed so you can get up you may go now." Connie was so mad.

Chapter 11

Mom was finishing up the flapjacks as all the kids were looking for Larry. she could see the older girls out in the pasture looking for me.

 The youngest kids were looking in front for Larry, plus the backyard.

Slowly they headed for the creek, When out of the bushes came a cougar, Josie looked at us all and yelled run! Run.!

Coming around the corner of the house was Darci at first she did not notice us running tell she heard Josie yelling but could not make out what she was saying.

 Jose looked over her shoulder and the cougar was gaining on them, run!!!!

 But before they knew it the cougar leaped and landed on Josie. Blair turned around looking for something to hit the cougar with but to her surprise out of nowhere was another cougar charging at Blair.

Darci ran to the ladder on the back porch climbing as fast as she could, leaving the sliding door open, But mom was not in the kitchen knocking hard on the door but she did not hear me.

Coming down the driveway was Albert he heard the yelling and ran to the back of the house, seeing what was going on he ran to the trunk of his car grabbed his gun, and ran back shooting the gun in the air 4 times. The Cougar, who was chasing Blair, turned around and ran back to the bushes.

Josie could not get the cougar off her fight for her life she yelled once more run to the house you too, just as they were running mom came out of her bedroom because she heard gunshots.

"What's going on?"

Darci was talking so fast mom could not understand her.

 "Slow down!" Mom replied

Running over to the sliding glass door she now saw what was happening, Albert started running down to help, not even opening the gate he jumped right over the fence.

 With his gun in one hand, he pulled the trigger and shot the cougar in the head by the time he got to Jose she was not moving and was breathing shallow.

Mom was running down to the pasture "yelling at the girls to get inside now!"

By the time she got to Jose she was not breathing "Abigaile call 911 for help!" Mom started CPR on Josie but it was not working, yelling out to God to save her, and asking where is the help.

 Just then you could hear the fire engine coming around the corner, Blair was out front to let them know where she was, the EMTs grabbing the oxygen tank and making a dash out to the pasture.

"You need to move so we can work on her." putting the oxygen mask on her she starts to breathe slowly.

The lady Parametric was checking her out to see if there were any broken bones. Turning her head she asks Man Parametric to go get the gurney, "Josie, please just lay still everything will be okay. " Mom Said.
 The Paramedic all helped to get me on the gurney, taking me up to the ambulance, and off she went to the Children Hospital, two weeks later she was back home being herself once again.

Chapter 12

As I was walking I started singing one of my favorite songs out loud "There a Lighthouse on the hillside that overlooks life seas."

 The sun was setting but I was determined to get to Oz before the end of the month. As it was slowly getting dark I noticed glowing rocks on the side of the road, this will help light the way at night.

Off in the distance, I could hear howling, Hoping it was not a wolf or coyote coming my way. Thinking to myself what if the wolves are like the wolf in Little Red Riding Hood that got me more scared than ever.

 I have got to find something to eat so I can keep my energy up and make it there.

Before long I came upon a bush full of raspberries, one of my all-time favorite fruits. In the back of my mind, I kept hearing the same thing. You better not touch it look what happen in the past with the pie tree and toast tree, But standing there looking at them made my mouth water. Maybe just one and then I will be on my way but before you knew it, I eat every last one on the bush, With the back of my hand I ripped my mouth and could not believe I did this, I was shaking in my pants.

 Looking around I did not see anybody or anything, I started a faster pass so I could be as far away from the raspberry bush before someone spotted me.

I'm so glad the rocks can light my way in the dark, up ahead I saw a little log cabin I wonder who lived here, the door was open maybe I will just take a peek inside and see if anyone's at home and ask them if I could get a drink of water, but it was so dark I could not see, I just remembered the glowing rocks off I ran to pick up two, running back to the cabin I stepped inside the glowing rocks lit up the whole room, Checking out this one-room cabin I saw a bed, a table with chairs around it and cabinet in the back of the cabin along with some dirty dishes and by the front door was a coat stand with one yellow coat on it. Oh my! I must be in the land of Winkies.

Coming up behind me was a short round fat man with a handlebar mustache.

"May I ask what are you doing in my cabin?" he yelled.

"I was thirsty from my walk and I saw a cabin in the distance and I wanted to ask the person that lived here if I could have a drink of water.

"Well, it doesn't mean you can just walk into someone's home when nobody inside." The round fat man replied angrily.

I walked out of the cabin and was about to leave when the man said you can have a drink of water from the barrel around the corner. I turned back around and walk around the cabin to where the barrel was, there was hooked on the barrel was a scoop for dipping into the water for a drink.

Walking back around the corner I stopped in front of the man and asked him "Am I in the land of Winkies

"Why do you ask?" replied the round fat man.

"Because I saw your yellow coat hanging on the coat rack."
He bowed his head and with a sad look on his face and replied
softly "No you are not."
"But I saw the yellow coat!" replied Larry
"I don't want to talk about this. Be on your way young man."
He walked back to his cabin and slammed the door. Bam!!
As you might be able to see, I did not make a very good first
impression. I felt sad about doing this. As I was walking away, I
decided to go back and apologize.
 As I walked up the path to the log cabin from the corner of my
eyes I could see a wolf standing on a boulder, just looking at me,
with his black bitty eyes my heart started beating so fast I
thought it would come up my throat.
I took a deep breath and slowly started for the cabin, but the
wolf slowly started to come. I saw in front of me a rock picked it
up and tried with all my might to hit the wolf in the head, but I
missed and hit an apple tree. Boy, do I have terrible aim. I better
not join a baseball team, otherwise, they will always lose.
Just before I came up to the door of the cabin I heard a voice
saying. "Watch where you're throwing that thing" I looked
around but did not see anybody.
 "I'm over here!" Said the voice. I turned in the direction that the
voice was coming from. It was coming from the direction of the
apple tree. I thought to myself. The tree can be the one that is
talking, trees can't talk.
 I thought someone was playing a joke on me, but then I
remembered what happened to Dorothy with the apple tree

talking and throwing apples at her. I remember that because I read it in the book and I watched the movie. I walked over to the apple tree and said to the tree "I thought you were in a different part of Oz when they hit Dorothy with apples."

"You are so right!" replied the apple tree

"Then what are you doing here?" replied Larry

"You see, the little fat man with handlebar mustache took an apple from one of these trees and when he got back home it took the seed and then planted it here." said the apple tree

"Oh! That makes a lot more sense."I said

"Well I better go," Walking back to the cabin I almost forgot about the wolf but lucky for me I made it just in time. After knocking a few times the little fat man finally opened the door.

"I thought I told you to be on your!" yelled the little fat man.

"I just came back to apologize," I replied

"Okay. Go ahead and apologize and then be on your way."

"Well, mister I am very sorry that I disturbed you and your day. I got done apologizing and the little fat man just slammed the door right in my face. That was rude of him, I thought.

When I turned around, there was a wolf, and standing by the wolf was a warlock in a black cloak with stars all over the cloak. In his left hand was a staff and on top of the staff was a black snake with brown spots it and it was wrapped around the staff. He had long grey hair with a hint of brown to it, also had a long beard that went down to his stomach, His eyes were the color of grey.

He walked with a limp and when he came closer I saw that he had a scar on his left cheek.

I just stood there not moving a muscle and looking him in the eyes.

"Where did you come from?" He said in a deep voice.

"I came from Lebanon, OR." Replied Larry

"Well, you entered the wrong part of Oz you are in the black hole" Replied the Warlock.

"But when I came threw the hole I landed in Pigment and papa pig told me to follow the yellow brick road tell I got to the Emerald City," replied Larry

"But did you ask which way on the yellow brick road you should have been takin?." The Warlock said.

With a tear coming down my cheek, I told him that nobody told me a different way to go. Thinking to myself I sure wish mom and dad were here to get me out of here.

Before I knew it the warlock picked up his staff and pointed it at me and the next thing I knew I was in a very small jail cell, looking around all I could see was walls except for a crack in the cement wall I went over and tried to see if I could see outside but all I could see was a blue fairy sitting on a stool in the darkness.

"Mommy come and get me please!!!!!!!!!!!!!!!!!!" yelling at the top of my lungs.

"Well, well how do you feel now?" replied the Warlock.

I could not get a word out because I was so frightened.

"I'll be back later." smoke covered the warlock and *POOF* he was gone.

Sitting in the corner I put my hands over my eyes and started crying and sniffling. From the crack, I heard in a small childlike voice saying "Don't be afraid." I got up and walked over to the crack in the wall but it was just the fairy talking to me.

"How did you get in jail," asked Larry

My brother and I were playing too close to the edge of the black hole. Mom always said never play this close but I did not listen and see what happens." the fairy said.

I felt so sad for her I almost cried but I held it in, "I'm so sorry this happened to you." replied Larry

"Tell me how you came here?" asked the fairy

I explained it all to her, And she just stood there looking at me through the crack in the cement. Just then I heard footsteps coming heavily around the corner and to my surprise, it was a lad. He didn't even notice me at first. He walked back to my cell and stood there eyeing me.

"Who are you?" the lad asked

"Larry."

"How did you come about being here?" replied the Lad

"Do you have a moment and I can tell you what happened from the beginning?"

"Well I have to get back to work, but I will try to make time for you." Sitting next to the bars the lad listen closely to every word I said, just as I got to the end of the story, an old lady was standing behind the lad, she looked very mean and her nose was so long it reminds me of the story about Pinocchio but on the end of her nose was a very large pimple.

"I have been looking all over the castle for you, and here you sitting talking to the prisoner, what do you have to say for yourself?"

The lad just looked up at her with no words to say. She reached down and grabbed the lad's ear and pulled him away.

As I sat there in my cell, I was trying to remember all the different turning points on the yellow brick road, wondering if I should have taken a different turn on the road and where would it lead me to.

Chapter 13

Weeks went into months and the only person I saw was the keeper of the Jail when it was time for meals.

I couldn't tell if it was night or day because I had no windows. To keep me busy I would do shadow puppets by the crack in the cement wall, the fairy could light up a room so I could have a shadow, we both spent our days talking.

It seems like I've been here for months. The funny thing was that my clothes weren't getting any smaller.

Then one day when I woke up and the lad was sitting by the bars of my cell.

"Good morning sleepy head." said the lad

I crawled over to the bars, and in a whisper, I asked: "What are you doing here?"

"I came to get you out of here?" replied the Lad.

Putting his hand in his hip pocket and he pulled out a small key.

I knew at that moment what the key went to. As the lad put the key in the lock it would not unlock. Standing right behind the lad again was the lady. She picked the lad up by the back of his neck, saying "What do we have here?" The lad dropped the key as if he was in a state of shock. without letting him answer, she slapped him upside his head. The blow was so hard that he fell to the ground. The thump could be heard down the hall.

I was just watching with my mouth opened She looked at me with a laugh that could chill your bones.

"You will never get out of here!!!!!" said the lady.

Just before she pulled him up off the floor he slowly reached for the key without her seeing him. Grabbing the lad by the ankle she pulled him over to the other side of the hallway and chained his arms and legs to the cement wall, turning around she left him there to die.

Just at that moment he realized she didn't lock the chains so quickly he went to the bar, in a whisper, "I still got the keys, she forgot to take them with her." said the Lad.

"But the last time you tried it didn't work," replied Larry.

"Cross your fingers hope it works this time." said the Lad. Turning the key very slowly, all at once the lock open with a click, I came out of the cell I whispered, "what about the fairy?" asked Larry.

That was my next stop, hopefully, the key works once again I turned in a different way and the locked open and fell to the ground with a thump, the fairy was so happy to be out, that she started to yell in a high pitch voice. I grabbed her and put her in my pocket, and told her "Sh Sh" we both were tiptoeing down the other side of the hallway as we go to the end of the hallway, I looked at Lad "Which way should we go?" said Larry.

"Let's go to the left that the old way of coming and going out." replied the Lad.

Going down the hallway I could hear moaning coming from the other cells I wanted to look in the peephole but the lad kept telling me. "We do not have time to be looking in all the cells or we will never escape from the castle!" replied the lad.

As we kept on going we were just about to go down the steps when two black cats startled us as they ran past us.

  We both started taking two steps at a time so we could get out of this gloomy castle. As we got to the last step we could see the door in front of us. The lad turned the knob, but the door would not open. I remember from a movie I saw that some people put the key above the door standing on my tiptoes reaching and hoping the key was there to my surprise the key was there. "Look what I found!" I exclaimed.

  The lad hugged me. I placed the key in the lock and it unlocked the door. But we had another problem, vines were blocking our way out.

"So what are we going to do? We have nothing to cut the vines with," ask Tom

 I was thinking about what to do next, "I got it we will just have to pull the vine out of our way and rip the vines so we can get out."

Working their hardest to get out we finally made it, we looked around and are surprised we saw two guards at the corner, trying our best not to let them see us we started to walk past them, we heard one of the guards snooze the other one was looking the other way, so we dashed into the woods just then the guard poked the other guard to wake him, the Lad had someone else with him are escaping the castle lets go get them.

We could hear footsteps come our way. "Hurry Larry!"

We keep running till we saw a log that went from one bank to another bank, I was scared to cross it because it was so high

above the river, the Lad was already walking across the log
when he yelled: "You have to do it or the guard will get you and
put us both in the cell."
With all my might I pulled myself up on the log and stood up
started walking across the log when I got to the end, both guards
were in the middle of the log walking sideways. I jumped off the
log yelled, "help me push this log into the river we keep trying
and trying to tell all of a sudden the log went into the water
splash the two-guard was trying to hang onto the log but the
river was moving to fast, they both stared floating away, as they
were float we could see an alligator swimming after them before
you knew it the alligator grabbed one of the guards and was
eating him.
 "Coming on! Just don't stand there like a lump of clay" said the
Lad.
I ran to catch up with the Lad and we were on our way once
again. I never have seen ravens so big before they were like the
size of a 7-pound chihuahua and had a wingspan of an eagle.
I was getting petrified with seeing so many ravens near us.
I didn't know if I should just stand still or just walk slowly
away, we both looked at each other and we both could tell what
the other was thinking. So slowly we walk tell us were over the
hill.
 It was getting much lighter than previously "So we must be
almost out of the black hole of Oz." said the Lad.

We keep a steady pace tell we were on the border of the black hole Oz. We both took one last look behind us then one big step in front of us, we made it out safe.

Chapter 14

We both keep on going a couple of feet when I felt a tickle in my pants pocket, I had forgotten about the fairy as soon as I took her out she wiggled her way lose out of my hands and started flying around us.

As she flew back in front of us we all heard a noise it flying to my left there was a group of fairies coming closer, then out of the middle of the group came a bright yellow fairy she flew straight to the blue fairy, "Trixie you are back!" she yelled. "Mom!!" replied Trixie.

This was my first time seeing fairies, I always thought they were just a fairytale or you saw them in a movie. Man would my family be surprised at all the different things I've seen on my journey.

 "So where are you going now that you got out of the castle?" asked.

"Well, I thought I could go with you to Emerald City so I could get back home also." Replied the lad

 "I thought you lived somewhere in Oz?" Said, Larry

"Oh no! I'm from Bremerton, WA" replied the Lad.

As they were walking up the hill, I asked: "How did you come to Oz?"

"I was at school and we had to do a book report so I decided to read The Wizard of Oz when I was done with the book and book report I was taking the book back to my school Library, but just as I push the door open the book fell out of my hands and open to the page where Dorothy helps the scarecrow out, Next thing I knew I was in Oz"

"So how did you end up in the black hole of Oz?"I asked
"I was trying to get to Emerald City but just like you, I went the wrong way and I thought the black Hole of Oz was dark because it was night time but to my surprise, it wasn't the mean lady you meet was coming back on a day journey out of the black hole of Oz and she grabbed me because I was a stranger to this part of Oz, she took me to the warlock and he made me a slave. I don't know how long I have been here and my parents probably gave up looking for me also." replied the lad.
"Well, you might as well come with me on my journey," I suggested
"Maybe I will." replied the lad.
"You must have a name, It can't be Lad," I said
"Tom."
We both looked at each other and laughed until we could not laugh anymore.
Gradually we were making some pace on our walk when we come to a fork in the road. There was a sign that read
    'Winkies land'
Tat was pointing to the right. There was another sign that was pointing to the left. It didn't have anything written on it.

Tom turned to me and asked, "Which way do you think we should go?"

"I'm not sure. I don't want to go the wrong way and end up in another part of the black hole."I replied.

"Same here!" said Tom

"Let's take a cat nap in the grass then we can decide what to do," I said

"Sounds like a good idea to me," replied Tom.

After their short nap, I said, "I think we should head to Winkies country."

"Are you sure?" Replied Tom

"How do we know? Winkies is the right way to go the other way might be, but do you remember reading about them in The Wizard of Oz book?" replied Larry.

They just took their first step when Tom stopped dead in his tracks "I have a strong feeling we should go the other way.

"But there is no sign telling us what city this is" Replied Larry.

"Please let's go back and see if the sign has fallen," suggested Tom.

"Okay if this makes you happy then I'm willing to go back and see." Replied Larry.

 They keep looking and looking but had no luck in finding A sign.

"We might as well just turn around and see if the Tin Man can help us get back home," said Larry.

"But I thought we were heading to the Winkies Country."Asked Tom

"I thought you read the books on The Wizard Of Oz and some of the others. Then you would have to know that the Winkies of Oz honored the Tin Man and made him a tin castle so he could rule over the Winkies." Replied Larry

"Oh!" said Tom

So we turned back around and headed in the direction we were going before.

"This place is so bright and yellow with all different shades of yellow, I never seen a place like this before, replied Larry

"Me neither," said Tom

As we were walking we could see homes, flowers and many other things in different shades of Yellow, these people heard us coming and because of being shy they all ran into their homes and place of work and shut the door you could hear the clicking of the doors being locked and they also shut their shutters. But the Winkies Kids that were outside playing ran and hid in the yellow berry bushes and or behind the trees,

This seemed odd to us as we were watching them do this. A few of the male Winkies were running to the tin castle to tell the Tin Man what was going on.

But as they were doing this they both slipped on a yellow pebble and landed flat on their backs. As we walked closer to them we noticed that they weren't moving a muscle. They were not moving because they wanted us to think that they were dead.

But we know better than this. Bending down we shook them but they tried not to move but could not help themselves we looked around and saw, women wearing yellow long dresses with a full pinafore and white bonnet, with black boots. Men wore black bib overalls with a yellow shirt and straw hats and black boots. All the women wore their hair in a bun and girls wore pigtails or ponytails, All men and boys had short hair.

As we were trying to help them, coming up behind us was the Tin Man, we were so startled by the voice behind us, that we jumped up so fast we lost are balanced and fell on our butt, we both were staring at the Tin Man in awe because we never saw a Tin Man up close like this, and he was so tall.

In a deep holer voice "Well, Well I see we have two newcomers in the Winkies Country" Said the Tin Man.

We both did not know what to say because we were in shock at what we saw, the Tin Man was so shiny you could see your face in the tin just like looking in a mirror.

Larry Finally had enough courage to say "Hi."

Tom was too shocked he still couldn't get a word out.

The two Winkies men got up and ran behind the Tin Man.

"Now, Now let not be afraid of these young people you can all come out and greet them."

One by one the doors and shutters open and the people came out of their homes and workplaces along with the kids coming from their hiding places outside.

Chapter 15

We didn't know if the Tin Man really could get us back home safely. I just want to get back home to mom and dad. I turned my head so that Tom did not see tears rolling down my face. I didn't want him to think that I was a baby. That wouldn't be very fun.

 As all of the people got closer to use they started making a circle around us.

"How did you get here?" Tin Man asked.

I told my story exactly as it happened. Then when it came to Tom, it took him a while to work up the courage to talk. He finally did and he told all of his stories, start to finish.

I looked at the Tin Man in the eyes and asked him, "Can you get us both home?"

"Why I might be able to help you but we need to go to the Emerald City and talk to the Lion and Scarecrow about this first, as we are all in charge of Oz." replied the Tin Man

"Then How can you rule over the Winkies then if you still have to talk to the other before getting us home." Asked Larry

The Tin Man was trying to think of how to say this so Larry would understand better, You see when the Wizard left Oz in his hot air balloon he put the Scarecrow, Lion, and I in charge tell the day he comes back, but it's kind of like I'm just a mayor over the Winkies, but working together with the other we are like one, we have to be together to talk things over, one of us can not change anything that is going to make Oz different unless we all think it's best for Oz." Replied the Tin Man.

"So it's kind of like when Dorothy came to Oz only the Wizard could say what to do so you three are like one big brain," I said.

"I never thought of it this way before but that good thinking." replied the Tin Man

"Are we going to go in a hot air balloon like the Wizard did when he left the Emerald City? Asked Tom

"I see you can talk, but it's getting kinda late for you both to be traveling now." Said the Tin Man

The city councilmen walked up to them we welcome you in the name of the Winkies county and gave each one of them a yellow stone necklace. Both of us boys said thank you.

"You may stay overnight in the castle." replied the Tinman. Coming through the crowd was a middle-aged lady with blankets and pillows, "You will need these to keep you warm. It gets mighty cold in the castle at night." I thought to myself, this must be the person that's been giving me the sleeping bags and blankets at night.

We both said are "Thank you for the blankets and pillows."

"Can I ask you something," replied Larry.

"Sure you can." With every eye on Larry, he spoke with a scratchy voice "Are you the one that keeps giving me blankets or sleeping bags at night."

"What do you mean?" asked the middle age lady.

Everybody waited for a reply. "Well you see whenever it was bedtime I found a blanket or sleeping bag there and I looked around in awe at this to see if someone was there, but nobody." The Tin Man started to talk slowly "You must be talking of the pixies they help people out that are under 13 years old, these pixies are different then most pixies, they do not have a home they just go wherever they want to and if they want to, they will help that person out."

It seems odd to me what I was hearing the Tin Man say. "But why can't I see them?" replied Larry

Before the Tin Man could get his words out, Tom spoke up "There is no such thing as fairies. That is just something they made up in the movies for little kids."

 All at once like a wave from the ocean you could hear the Winkies laughing, they knew different.

Turning around I looked at Larry and asked: "Why are they laughing at me."

 "It's what you said about the pixies not being real," replied Larry.

 "Will I always thought it was something people made up," said Tom.

  "Well Tom now what do you think of pixies now?" replied the Tin Man in a strong deep voice.

  "Then why didn't Larry ever see the pixies?" Asked Tom

"Sometimes they do not want people to see them, they just want to be nice. Do you believe in Santa Claus Tom?

 "sure! Who doesn't believe it? " Replied Tom

"That my point people can't see Santa Claus? but they believe they put cookies and milk out on Christmas Eve for him". Said the Tin Man.

You could till Tom was getting what the Tin Man was saying because of the smile on his face.

We were both getting tired and hungry, one of the ladies Winkies came forward, "You both are welcome to have dinner at our house if you like."

One of the little Winkies kids said: "You better take my mom up on her offer you will not find any food at the castle unless you like eating different types of oil."

"Ewe Yukie!!!!" Larry and Tom said

We both accept the invitation to dinner with delight, We started to follow right behind her when the Tin Man Replied I "will see you after dinner."

Larry said with a happy sounding voice "Yes you will!"

As the boys came closer to the home they could smell the aroma of the roast coming out the open Window.

"Come on in make yourself at home." The middle-aged lady said.

Walking into the home was a surprise to us because we never saw a fountain in someone living room that had fish in it before. The table was set with everything of yellow even the silverware was yellow in the middle of the table was a vase that held sunflowers. The middle-aged lady turned back around and spoke with a soft voice. "You all can sit at the table now my husband should be walking in the door at any minute before her last word came out the door opened up.

 "Honey I'm home!"

Looking straight ahead he notices the two boys at the time. "I see you invited the new visitor to dinner that was very kind of you Mandy." Replied the Husband.

 We felt like kings because of all the food on the table and trying our best to be polite when he asked us if we would like some sunflower wine.

Both of us not giving it a second thought, held up the wine glass as he poured each glass full. "Thank you." Both at the same time replied.

As we sat around the table with our new friends we just made we felt happy and safe. They asked us how we came to Oz and we both told them our story. They wanted to know more about us, but time was slipping by so fast when the bell went off Mandy's Husband took out his pocket watch it was 8:30 and the sun was going down.

"Well, I better walk you to boys to the castle before it gets too late."

"Does that bell go off at 8:30 every night?" Asked Tom.

"Sure does, this makes sure everyone is safe at home before it gets dark."

We said our goodbyes and walked out the door when Mandy Husband picked up a torch and lit it, this made it easier to see in the dark.

We were still in awe at what has happened so far and we keep looking around and could see the homes where are lighted up on the guitar like they had Christmas Lights on.

"How come everyone has Christmas lights hanging around their gutters." Asked Tom

" Not Christmas Light there yellow lights for are Founder Day next week." replied the Husband.

With both did not know what Founder Day was at the same time both boys asked: "What is Founder Day."

"It's the day we celebrate when we became free from the wicked witch of the West, the Winkies are very happy about what Dorthy did for us. If it was not for her we might still be under her powers and be working for her for every, that why we put yellow lights up.

"Then whatever happened to the flying monkeys?" Replied Larry.

"They're still around." replied the husband.

When we got to the castle the husband rang the bell twice to let the Tin Man know someone was here, from the corner window we saw a Winkie waving to let us know he heard the bell slowly the draw bridge opened. As we were walking on the drawbridge we could see a moat around the castle, we both looked at the other and knew what the other was thinking, Hopeful there know alligators in the water.

As we walked into the castle we could feel the cold, lucky we had both had a blanket to keep us warm tonight, coming you could hear loud thumping coming down the hallway it was the Tin Man.

 Let me show you around the castle, First room he showed us was where he sat on the throne, it was a big room he showed us all the rooms when we got to the kitchen you could see tons of oil cans.

 "Let me show you to your bedroom." said the Tin Man.
The room was kind of bland I could not believe my eyes there was a tin bed with a tin pillow there was a picture hanging above the bed it was of the Scarecrow, Lion, Dorothy, Toto and the Tin Man on the yellow brick road there was a window in the room.
"If you get cold there are a blanket and a pillow I keep these for people that are not made of Tin," Said the Tin Man with a smile."
"Thank You."Replied Larry
"Tom your room is next door." said the Tin Man.
When I got there everything was the same except for the picture it showed them standing in front of the Emerald City.
We both didn't think we sleep on a tin bed because it would be so hard, but we both manage to.

Chapter 16

The sunshine came into our room covering our face with beams of light that woke us up to the sound of birds chirping.

As we both sat on the edge of the bed stretching before putting on our shoes.

We both opened the bedroom doors at the same time, we both heard each other's door opened we both started laughing.

Coming out of the bedroom door the tips of our shoes touch the tray that had food on it.

Larry looked at Tom "I wonder where the food came from?"

"Who cares let's just eat, I'm hungry."

Larry looked straight at Tom "looking over by the window there's a round table and two chairs let go eat there."

Picking up their trays they hurried over to the table.

"I never had Egg Benited before Always wanted to try it," said Tom

"Me too" looking at Tom "My mom would never have bacon and Sausage both for breakfast," Larry said

We could not grasp how much food was on our plates and saucers, in a little dish was fruit cocktail, a glass of milk, and tea.

Once again we could hear thumping on the tin floors. Before we knew it the Tin Man was standing right in front of us.

"Good morning young fellows did you guys sleep well last night."

"Well you see we are not used to sleeping on a tin bed are beds soft, but it kind of like sleeping out on the ground when you go camping." Replied Larry

"I see, I wanted to ask you guys a question I would like to go with you when you leave to go to Emerald City I have not seen the Scarecrow and the Cowardly Lion in awhile

Both didn't know they were saying it loud, why sure!!

After breakfast, the Tin Man went to get his oil can from the kitchen and hook it to his side so he would not have to carry it in his hands.

"Before we go I need to tell the Winkies I'm going on a journey. Said the Tin Man

As they came to the draw bridge the Tin Man rang the bell and all the Winkies came to the castle.

Standing on the draw bridge the Tin Man-made spoke I will be going on a trip to the emerald city with these young boys so I can visit my friends, as I'm gone I will have my helper be in charge tell my return they all waved and said their goodbyes.

Chapter 17

"We were having a Jolly time on our journey the Tin Man told
us his story of how he became a Tin Man.

And we told him about our family and where we came from and
what our parents did for a living.

"I bet you miss them dearly." said the Tin Man

At the same time with tears coming down our cheeks and having
trouble getting the words out. "We sure do miss our parents."

"I now miss my brother and sister even if they can be a pain in
the butt at times," said Larry

"Do you have any brothers or sisters Tom?" asked the Tin Man

 "No, I'm an only child," replied Tom.

After hours of walking, Tom and I were getting tired. Our legs
were starting to hurt. We both asked the Tin Man if we could
stop the rest for a little bit. He replied let keep walking till we
come up to that log up yonder then you both will have a place to
sit.

We both replied that sound good to me, finally we made it we
were so happy to stop walking. As far as the eye could see we
saw trees of different types of fruit on the other side of the
yellow brick road was a beautiful waterfall.

Without thinking about my family back home, " I sure would
like to live right here for every it the prettiest place I ever saw."
Said, Larry

"What about you Tom? Asked the Tin Man

"It's is a nice place to visit but I would much prefer to be home with dad and mom.

The sun was setting over the waterfall it looked so peaceful. The Tin Man walked over to the mango tree and pulled off two mangoes and then walked over to grab some bananas for dinner.

 We were all tired except for the Tin Man I guess he never gets tired because he's made of Tin. before we knew it, it happens once again there were two sleeping bags and two pillows right at the end of our feet.

As we rolled out the sleeping bags there was a piece of candy wrapped up picking up the candy and opened the wrapper slowly we put the candy in our mouth the taste was so wonderful and creamy going down our throats.

 Each of us got into our sleeping bag it felt like we were laying on feathers it was so soft before our heads hit the pillow we were already asleep.

 As we woke up we didn't see the Tin Man around, Tom looked at me with a scared look on his face.

"Do you think the Tin Man left us because we had to sleep and he did not need the rest like us?" Ask Tom

"I'm not sure, but let's get up and go get a drink of water before we have our breakfast as we were walking you could hear someone whistling some distance away.

We did not know if we should go see where the whistling was but we both wanted to know where it was coming from maybe this is where the Emerald city is located. But what if it is not and this is someone's way to get us back to the Black Hole of Oz so instead we just keep going till we got to the stream.

"So I see you guys are up and about I was wondering when you would wake up."

 Tom turned around just as I did and asked did you hear the whistling as he points to where it was coming from.

"Oh, that was just me getting our breakfast and you did not even see the basket I'm holding full of fruit."

Placing the basket beside them we start taking the fruit out we saw different kinds of fruit that we had never seen before as one looked like an apple but it was the size of watermelon but the inside tasted like bananas and cherries.

After the smoochies fruit breakfast got another drink of water, but before we left the Tinman ask "Can you please oil my knee, elbows, and neck.

Tom grabbed the oil can and did what was requested by the Tin Man.

Tom looked over his shoulder and asking Larry "I hope it's not much further I would just like to sleep in my bed and be able to play with my cat again,"

The Tinman was starting to cry "now look what you made me do?"

We both looked at his face tears were coming down his cheek, I remember when I saw the Wizard of Oz movie and he was starting to cry Dorothy told him to stop crying or he would rust again.

"Please don't cry or you will rust and be standing here for a very long time." Said, Larry

The Tin Man Just remember the last time this was said to him it was when Dorothy and the Scrowcrow found him in the apple orchard

I found a hanky in my pocket and gave it to the Tin Man to wipe away the tears.

 After some time the Tin Man was ready to go as we got to the top of the hill, we could see the glowing of Emerald City of in the distance there.

Tom and I jump up and down yelling Yippee!!!!!!

I looked at the Tin Man and asked him, "Where are all the poppies are."

"They are on the other side of the Emerald City before you get to the front door, we are going in the back door."

It seems like forever before we got to the back door we saw a button so I let the Tin Man push it a loud bell went off and a lady looked through a small hole in the door, she opened the door and we walked in.

"Been a long time since I have seen you, and I see you have a couple of people with you."

"Yes, they need to get back home so I need to see the lion and scarecrow so we can talk about how to get them home as soon as we went down the step everyone turned around because you could not help but hear the Tin Man when he walked.

 Coming from the crowd was the Scarecrow and the lion.

Both the scarecrow and lion said, "Been a long time it's nice to have you back."

"Likewise."

The Tin Man introduce Tom and Larry and told everyone how they came to Oz and they need to get home.

 "Come with us we'll show you how to get home see that chair there that green and white just go take turns sitting there and just say please take me home.

But I need to ask about the reporter that went to the sandland I heard there a story on the radio but I never got to hear how it ended. Before you knew it the reporter was standing in front of me and I asked: "what happens after you cleaned the water tower."

"Well you see the next day they help fix the helicopter and we left and now we are home.

Larry was the first one to sit down said his goodbyes and said please take me home.

Chapter 18

Then the next thing I felt was my brother jumping on me, I yelled I'm back home, everybody came running into our bedroom.

Mom asked, "What is going on here!"

"I came back home!" said Larry

Blair said, "You never left."

Yes, I did and I told them what happened my mom told me to lay back down and rest.

But then I remembered the soap flack candy I look over the edge of my bed and there it was I showed them and turn the box around so they could see the stamp of Oz showed them yellow necklace I had on the other side said just tap the yellow rock 3 time and ask if you can come back to OZ it will say yes or no or maybe try later.

They were surprised, I looked around and asked, "Where's Josie"?

The first book in the series is just the beginning of the great adventures of the Family of Oz. In this book, you will journey through Oz with Larry, a young boy from Lebanon, Oregon